W9-DDW-822

CONSIDER THIS

BEFORE

HAVING A CHILD

*

Child Rearing
Seeds for Thought

The intent of this book is *not* to give advice but rather, is a means of sharing thought provoking seeds to encourage personal development for today's young adult.

This is part of   The Book Series to Consider

Though not endorsed by Shepherd's Chapel references made are with permission.

Printed in the United States of America

ISBN 978-0-9777851-0-0 this book

ISBN 978-0-9777851-6-2 four biblical book set

Coming soon   www.publishinggodsway.com

To contact us   publishinggodsway@bv.net   or
352-391-1959

Consider This before Having a Child

My Gift to You

Occasion

From

Date

Dedication

This book is dedicated to my son Gary and daughter, Jodi who were my inspiration to offer something to today's young adult.

Raising them as a single parent, I often thought they did not hear one word I said however, if they had to prove me wrong in any one area of their lives, I am glad they chose this one.

I am very proud that they have taken their time to develop who they are and who they want to be.

I will always encourage each of them to have a close relationship with God, to always hold their head up high, to set and accomplish their goals, as well as to live an honest, fulfilling life and be the very best that they can be before becoming responsible for a child!

Am I ready to devote twenty years or more
of my life to this child?

Acknowledgements

I sincerely thank my sister Noni and her husband Wayne for their sympathetic ears and all of their support through the difficult years of raising my children on my own.

I thank my brother Jon for his support, encouragement, advice and guidance through those same years and I send a very special thank you to Paula and Roger, my closest and very dear friends who have been by my side through many of the hills and valleys of my life.

I thank my dear friends (Margit, Donna, Jan, Charlene, Joanne and Dot) who have all remained in my life after my late husbands' death more than twenty six years ago and I sincerely thank my husband Frank as it was his love and support that has made this book possible!

How tired do I want to be?

Authors' Note

My mother and father at eighteen years old were children raising their first child and my husband and I at nineteen years old were children raising our first child.

At twenty four years old I had a husband and two children and at twenty nine I was widowed (after an accident took my husband) leaving me to raise my nine year old son and five year old daughter on my own with no college, little money and so tired!

Although some years as a single parent were more challenging than others it was the teenage years which caused me the greatest concern as I was worried that my children would have a child before they were ready (emotionally, physically and or financially).

Rather than give them a very long speech, being sure that they would tune me out. I needed an *impact* statement that would prevent them from adding unnecessary difficulties to their lives while they were so young.

The statement I made was; "Before you even consider bringing a child into the world, ask yourself one question. *"Am I ready to devote twenty years or more of my life to this child?"*

Their jaws dropped, as they had never given it a *thought*. Why would they? They were about seventeen and thirteen when I sprung this on them!

Today, neither of my children (at thirty-five and thirty one) has a child, and for a very good reason.

They are still growing up themselves, developing who they are and who they want to be. So right now, they are living their lives for themselves!

They come and go as they want, sleep or get up when they want and are free to make decisions based on what they would like to do rather than having to consider the needs of a young child first.

So, before you even consider having a child, ask yourself one question. *"Am I ready to devote twenty years or more of my life to this child?"*

The exclamation marks throughout this book are an expression of my love, passion, enthusiasm and devotion toward helping all of God's children, and yes, that means you!

Read this book with a friend and take advantage of the notes pages.

These pages have been provided for your convenience to encourage interactive discussions with those in your life, while allowing you to record thoughts of your own.

Introduction

This book was written, to plant some *seeds* for *thought* as to what is involved in raising a child.

If this book prevents one young person from having a child before she is prepared then I am glad I committed the time to writing it.

This book is for all children, young and old, rich and poor, those from happy homes and those from not so happy homes, those with children and those without children. This book was written for all who were told of the commitment of raising a child and chose to have a child anyway.

Now they cannot understand why a few years later they are so tired and at such a young age!

Give this material some *thought* before bringing another child into the world and remember, we can learn from books what we have not been taught at home or school.

Or we can learn from books what others have tried to *teach* us but we were not ready to *listen* to at the time.

A plan for your future is not taught in schools and in many cases is not taught at home either, so take charge of your life to develop who you are first, before committing twenty years or more of your life to raising a child, because:

A child is for the rest of your life!

Consider the absentee father.

Will the child's father be around next month or next year? Have you considered how difficult it will be raising a child on your own? Could you handle the responsibility by yourself?

If you are not married do you know that your mate is free to leave at a moments notice? Do you think he will have regrets (in some cases) leaving you with the responsibility and expense of raising his child?

These situations are rampant, especially in poorer neighborhoods where many have not been fortunate enough to be blessed with a good education.

Now *think* about this!

NOTES

Consider affordable housing.

Do you read the newspaper or watch the news to understand that the availability of affordable housing is very limited?

Have you asked questions of young people around you who are trying to make ends meet while living on their own? Would you have to live with a friend? Would your mate or roommate be reliable? Have you considered the cost of rent alone, not to mention all necessary living expenses?

Now consider the added expense that comes with raising a child!

Although at fifteen you are not ready to live on your own, one day you will and you will still be caring for your child.

NOTES

Story

Recently, my husband and I were looking to buy a home that was rented to a family with six young children.

This family was paying less than seven hundred dollars a month in rent when apartments of this size were renting for twelve hundred a month.

Now *think* about this!

This family had a good deal for the seven years they lived there but guess what happened when someone bought the house they were renting for a home of their own?

Even well intentioned, responsible parents have housing problems!

NOTES

Consider how you treat others.

Are you angry? How do you manage your anger? Did you grow up in an angry environment? Would you be offering your child an angry environment? Is it possible that an angry parent could raise an angry child? Of course it is!

Think about this! How can you raise a happy child if you are not happy?

Have you considered investing in yourself to diffuse the anger before investing the twenty or more years of your life to raising a child?

Children are not born angry but become angry through example and or environment. A happy child would be so much easier to handle not to mention that you will be far less tired!

NOTES

Story

We were at the home of some friends one day while their four-year-old son was there.

It was very clear to see in the first few minutes that this child was filled with anger. Why? And at such a young age!

The child was threatening to throw a rock at us as we stood talking in a group and it was quite apparent that the parents were tired and did not even know what to do.

We learned later that the parents were living in a very angry situation and unfortunately, this had passed on to the little boy.

Are they aware of what their anger has done to their son, who does not even understand what he is feeling?

How will this child grow to be a happy person when he is surrounded by anger and is now filled with it himself?

Now picture yourself either trying to undo the damage to this child or continuing in this current situation and trying to handle this angry child for the next fifteen or twenty years.

NOTES

Consider the angry teen-ager.

What kind of teenager are you or were you?

Do you believe that when you reach sixteen or eighteen years old that your parents can no longer tell you what to do? Do you believe that house rules no longer apply to you? Do you carry with you that "*know it all*" attitude?

Do you respect your parents and therefore trust that your child will respect you? On the other hand, when with friends, are you constantly venting about that which makes you angry?

Is it possible that an angry person has a distorted view of the world as well as life situations? Anger clouds your thinking. Now, add a child to the equation. Do you *think* it might be wise to take a few years to diffuse your anger first?

NOTES

Consider marriage.

It is not old fashioned to marry before having a child but rather it is God's way to marry before having a child!

There was a time (not too long ago) when couples dated, discussed their future, married, had children, raised their family and then grew old together.

Oh my! What a concept! Imagine!

What has happened through the years?

Even if you think that everyone else is doing it (having a child without being married) does not make it right!

Guess what? It is not God's way!

Something to *think* about isn't it?

15

NOTES

Story

A teenager once told her mother that she was the coldest, hardest person she knew.

While her mothers first, momentary thought was to burst into tears she decided to explain the difference between her daughter's perception of who she was and her own perception of herself.

This is what her mother had to say. "I was born to a large family and had to be strong to survive. Then at the age of nineteen, I had to have strength to survive a very difficult marriage and the last few years I have had to be strong every single day of my life to survive two angry rebellious teenagers!"

"You see, I am not cold or uncaring but I am of *strong will;* because up to the present, life has not allowed me the opportunity to be weak or gentle."

Her daughters reply was, "Now that you put it that way, I feel bad." Oh my! The power of communication!

That was a conversation that I had with my own daughter!

NOTES

Consider baby-sitting first.

Would you like to have someone else's child overnight for a week or month at a time?

Baby-sit first, off and on for a year or two and for a number of different children.

When you do baby-sit, is it for the money, or because you genuinely enjoy children?

This would be a good test to determine how patient you are and would be helpful to determine if having a child right now would be for you.

Once having a child of your own, there are no weekends off or days off or moments off without considering the needs of your young child!

Something worth thinking about!

NOTES

Story

We know some grandparents who were babysitting their four year old granddaughter who has not been taught the meaning of the word *no*. This child has been taught that a toy would be bought for her at every store they enter and if she screams loud enough and long enough they will stop at her favorite fast food restaurant for lunch.

When the grandparents shared with me the child's behavior I was quick to say, "I pity the man who marries her." Do you *think* this behavior will carry on into adulthood? Of course, it will! Why? Because she has not been taught any better!

The grandparents cannot teach the child what they have not yet learned!

Good behavior is rewarded and unruly behavior is not!

NOTES

Consider birth control.

Girls, absolutely *do not* leave this up to the man! How much have you heard about single fathers raising their children? Although there are some, there are not many by comparison!

Girls, women, females, birth control is your responsibility and do not be foolish enough to *think* that a pregnancy cannot happen to you!

Just ask the many parents out there who were not *thinking* of having a child!

Have you ever heard the phrase, "You play, you pay?" And! You pay for a very long time!

Now consider the long term consequences here!

NOTES

Consider child support.

Do you ask questions of relatives and friends? Do you ask questions of friends of friends about child support and how this works? Do you know that the formula used by the court is based on your gross salary (actual salary) and not your net salary (amount taken home after taxes)?

Do you know that when one young man asked the judge, "But how will I live?" (Most of his take home salary went to the child's mother), the judge answered that he did not care!

Do you know how many young fathers need to work two jobs to pay child support? There are many, so men and young men *think* about this! Some men pay child support for fifteen or twenty years and this is a very long time!

NOTES

Consider your childhood.

Through the years each of us acquires a history, some better or happier than others.

As we enter the role of young adult, we may have some issues that need working out. We may be angry with a parent or both!

We may have trouble communicating feelings or thoughts; however, as we mature we have the ability to correct this!

Keep this thought in mind: "Your parents did the best they could, no matter how good or bad you feel about their parenting skills!"

You cannot go back to fix the past but you can provide for a better future for yourself and your children by reading!

Read everything you can get your hands on (including the old King James Bible) that will help you with all of your life situations!

NOTES

Consider that children are to be seen and not heard.

Do you know that some children are raised in this type of environment? Is it because they have bad parents? No, but rather because their parents do not know any better.

Do you know that the child misses so many of the fundamentals of life and grows up to be very confused?

How can a child learn about communication and expression, negotiation and compromise, if they are pushed aside and are not allowed to have a voice or to ask questions?

If a child is not allowed to ask questions, then how will things be explained to her or him along life's road?

NOTES

Consider this man's story.

He was married twenty years, had four children and his wife filed for divorce because she was having an affair.

In addition to the ex-wife keeping the house, the court mandated child support in the amount of twelve hundred dollars per month and the support continued for eight years, so do the math!

Over eight years this man paid his cheating ex-wife over one hundred thousand dollars for child support. He lost his home, a good portion of his income and family life as he knew it?

For all you males reading this book find out how the fathers are treated through the courts when it comes to child support. The innocent husband was punished and the cheating ex-wife rewarded!

NOTES

Consider when a child has a bad day.

Do you think a child will always behave the way you would want him or her to?

How would you handle a child who throws tantrums? How would you handle the tantrum in public or at home?

Have you ever looked around you when out in public to observe the mothers who are tired and not from lack of a good night sleep but rather from trying to handle an unruly child day after day and year after year?

Just as we have bad days, children have bad days also and sometimes more than we would like them to have!

It could be easier if you mature, read and just take the time to develop who you are first!

NOTES

Consider the commitment.

This is not a temporary commitment, but rather, is a lifelong commitment. The commitment will continue day after day, week after week and year after year.

Bringing a child into the world is for the rest of your life will require a considerable amount of your time.

Develop who you are first and read everything you can get your hands on that will help you with your own growth and development.

Otherwise, the child and you could suffer needlessly!

There are no vacations from raising a child because a child is for the rest of your life!

NOTES

Consider a day care.

Will you have to work full time? Will you have to place the child in daycare?

Think about this! The child will be spending more time in day care than with you!

She or he may be in daycare for forty or more hours per week!

Now, I do not intend for this statement to sound as though I am opposed to daycare. I am not! However, this is something to consider, as a child learns so much more from being with adults than she or he could ever learn from other children!

Now consider this schedule long term whereby, you will have to drop the child off five mornings a week and pick up the child five afternoons per week before going home from work!

NOTES

Consider the crying child.

How would you handle this? Now, look within yourself to see how you would handle this long term if the child cried for hours at a time and day after day.

A baby communicates through crying when colic, sick or when needing love and attention.

Look at the sad situations (on the news) that have taken place through the years because a frustrated parent could not handle a crying child.

These situations are so sad, for both the child and the parent!

Babies cry whether being raised in a happy or unhappy home. Are you ready for this?

Take time to consider this!

NOTES

Consider not having a child until you are older.

Why? To give yourself time to develop who you are and who you want to be. Do this for yourself, as this could be the greatest gift that you could ever give to yourself and your future child!

Take time to mature to be better able to handle the commitments involved with raising a child.

So many young women and men today go straight from being a child under their parent's roof to raising a child with no time in between for herself or himself.

Have you ever given thought to the kind of life you may have, not to mention the freedom, if you wait to have a child until you are older?

NOTES

Consider depression.

Have you thought about how you feel during the lowest times in your life?

Have you considered how you would cope with taking care of yourself to be better able to care for your child?

Depression often worsens through the years as one takes on more responsibility and without the help of the Lord there is not much hope to correct this!

Young children can be very demanding so you must consider how you would handle this long term.

The answer to depression is God; not drugs!

Do you *think* you could handle this with patience and love?

NOTES

Consider children from different fathers.

There are many young, unmarried mothers with two or more children having different fathers.

Why, you wonder? Do you *think* it is because of their love of children, or do you *think* it is because they just did not take the time to *think* of the consequences?

Have you considered the conflicts that could arise due to fathers having different ideas about parenting?

Do you *think* your children will have added difficulties in school because they have different last names?

There does not appear to be a lot of kindness in the schools these days. Something to *think* about now isn't it?

NOTES

Consider the free man.

My son brought home a friend one day, who with a great deal of pride, was telling me that he fathered two children with two different young women, again proudly stating that he is always there if they need something!

What he meant was he buys them an occasional pair of sneakers!

He does not pay child support and justifies this with he cannot afford to! Outrageous!

He doesn't have time to be a dad because he is busy pursuing his own interests!

In addition, he does not live with his children so guess who is raising them?

Come on girls! Don't buy into this. It is not God's way!

NOTES

Consider discipline.

What is your idea of discipline? Will the discipline be with love and will it be consistent?

If a child is not disciplined, how much will she or he learn about boundaries? Do you know that discipline should not be nor does it need to be physical?

You would be surprised at what a child learns when time is taken to explain all the questions and issues along life's road!

A child needs to understand that some behavior is acceptable and some is not and that unacceptable behavior will have consequences.

Explanations help a child much more than punishment! How beautiful!

NOTES

Consider divorce or a relationship that ends.

Do you think it cannot happen to you? What if it does? Will you have to work the rest of your life while raising your children?

Will you have to struggle? Give some *thought* to the many struggling, single parent households out there! Consider not only how difficult a divorce or separation would be but add to this situation a child or more.

There are no guarantees in life so if we just pay attention and take the time to develop who we are first we could allow ourselves an easier life journey. It is just incredible what a little planning and self education could do for you!

Self education! What a concept!

NOTES

Consider educating yourself.

If college is not for you or you cannot afford the cost, there is another type of education. After school or work, stop by the library or a good bookstore several times a week and read everything you can that will help you handle all of life's situations.

Remember, the library is free. What a wonderful way to get a free education!

You do not even have to buy the books but you can read everything available on having and raising children. What a nice way to spend a few hours a week!

Do you *think* you will be better able to explain everything the curious child takes the time to ask?

This is where the child's foundation for a good life will begin!

NOTES

Consider encouraging the child.

Do you know how many children grow up in an environment where they are not encouraged to do or to be any better?

There is a great big world out there with so much to offer. Let me encourage you! Live first, self educate and have a child later!

I used to tell my children, "If there is anything you'd like to try or do and it is legal then go do it!"

If you want to read God's Word, take up golf, tennis, biking or whatever then go do it! If you want to take a few courses then go do it!

Live now, develop who you are and have children later!

NOTES

Consider the child's environment.

Can you offer your child a happy home? Do you have happy people around you, meaning friends and family?

Is the environment that you have to offer a child, an environment that you would have liked to have grown up in yourself?

If you do not enjoy your present environment, why would you want to bring a child into it?

Environment is important, friends!

Rich or poor doesn't matter! But Godly and tranquil does!

What a beautiful thing to be able to offer a child a peaceful environment, filled with love!

NOTES

Consider errands and trips to the grocery store.

Unless you have another responsible adult at home, you will have to take the youngster everywhere you go!

Every errand you do, nap you take or person you visit requires thought about the well-being of your child first!

Yes, rain or shine! Happy or crying!

It is not easy to work all day, pick up the child from daycare, do an errand or two and then arrive home to cook dinner and do a few household chores before turning in for the night!

Now ask yourself, how tired do I want to be? And for how long?

NOTES

Consider this situation.

You worked all day and rushed to daycare to pick up your little one who is teething and crying. It is raining outside and you have three stops before going home. You are taking the youngster in and out of the car with the baby seat in the rain and the baby is crying.

You arrive home an hour or so later and guess what? Now you have to cook dinner and the child is still crying. Oh, and the maid did not show up to do the dishes so guess who is going to wash them?

You put your little one to bed and now your day has ended at nine pm. Guess what?

You can get up tomorrow to do it all over again!

NOTES

Consider feeling trapped.

Your friends are going out to have a good time and you cannot go because you have the responsibility of caring for your child.

Freedom as you once knew it is now a thing of the past. Every move you make involves considering your child first.

You feel there are not enough babysitters around or not enough money to pay them and you are upset that you have to miss so much fun.

You may feel trapped and are becoming resentful of your situation!

While young, live, learn and diffuse any anger that you may have to better develop who you are and who you want to be, before having a child!

NOTES

Consider your finances.

A young male friend of my daughter told me he wanted to have six children and I asked him; why?

He said, because he loved children, (a nice response) however, I asked him if he has ever considered the cost and he asked what I meant.

I responded with, daycare is two hundred dollars per week or more, formula, baby food and diapers are another one hundred dollars per week. Not to mention doctor visits, toys and clothes and baby sitters if you want to go out occasionally and college costs.

Then I asked him if he had three hundred dollars per week that he did not know what to do with and he said, "Well no, I only make ten dollars per hour!"

On this, he supports the rent, utilities, car, etc. He wants six children remember?

The next day I asked my daughter if he was upset with what I had to say and she said "no" and that he felt quite the opposite.

When I asked what she meant she said that when they left he told her that be loved talking to me because I made so much sense.

All I did was plant a seed to have him *think*!

NOTES

Consider how you will feel after five, ten or more years!

Now yes, things do change as the child grows. At five years old a child is not teething but now you are working with other developmental issues!

A child is so much more than a cuddly, bundle of joy.

A child deserves love, understanding, protection, your time and a happy home environment with a very strong foundation to prepare her or him for our changing world!

Without some pre-planning, this for some becomes quite an exhaustive task!

Some talking, planning and reading can help tremendously in lessening some of life's burdens!

NOTES

Consider how frustrating raising a child can be!

When you consider the points already mentioned in this book as well as those not yet mentioned or those not mentioned at all, the unnecessary frustrations can mount!

Why unnecessary? Thought, pre-planning and education can help to minimize the frustrations!

The time to consider whether you are prepared to have a child is *before* planting those seeds of life and not after!

When you are not sure about something, reach out to God because He will not help us unless we ask!

Let God be your mentor as He will always lead you in the right direction! This way, you cannot make a mistake!

NOTES

Consider teaching your child to give.

This is an area neglected by so many. We get so caught up on the every day things and are on a lifelong mission of giving to our children that without realizing it we have only taught our children to take!

The evidence is all around us in the many selfish and or self-centered adults and children in the world!

Some are of the attitude that their partner is in their life to continue giving to and doing for them and they give very little or nothing in return!

Our Lord said that it is more blessed to give than to receive!

What a beautiful way to live one's life; trying to help others, such as is the purpose of these small books!

NOTES

Story

My husband and I had some friends over one weekend and my girlfriend was telling me that she was cleaning homes part time for a few millionaires.

She said there were surveillance cameras everywhere and that when the homeowners left to spend time at another of their homes the cleaning crew was instructed to throw all of the food in the refrigerator and freezer in the trash! Imagine!

The cleaning crew was not allowed to donate the food to the poor nor to food banks. The freezers were full of hundreds of dollars worth of meat and everything was trash bound. Why would they do this? Perhaps they have only learned to take all of their lives and have never learned the joy of giving. How sad?

NOTES

Consider goal setting.

This is something not even mentioned by a majority of parents, yet it is so important.

If a child is taught when young to set and reach small goals imagine what she or he will accomplish through the years while setting and reaching larger goals.

There is only one thing that builds self-esteem and one thing only, and that is *accomplishment*!

Start small and then continue to set goals throughout your life and see what happens.

No one else can build your self-esteem except you!

Now *think* about this as it certainly can be life altering!

NOTES

Consider being grounded the rest of your life!

An acquaintance of mine had a sixteen-year-old daughter who was pregnant when her fourteen-year-old brother said, "Are you nuts? It will be like being grounded for the rest of your life!" Imagine that?

This statement came from the lips of a fourteen-year old boy. Wise for his young years wasn't he?

What does grounded mean? Usually it means that you lose your freedom to come and go as you wish!

Yes, I think this young boy had a point because, unless his sister has someone reliable to care for the child; life as she has known it as a carefree teen, will now be a thing of the past!

NOTES

Consider that we can handle almost anything-short term!

Short term is easy! Why? Because we know that it will come to an end in the near future, making it (whatever it is) more bearable!

Long term is different! Why? It seems never ending! You go to bed tired and wake up tired and there just doesn't seem to be any rest for the weary!

So when considering having a child, it would be wise to ponder if you could handle the commitment for the rest of your life!

Remember, it is how we handle what we go through that matters!

So *think* about this! You cannot get any more long term than for the rest of your life!

NOTES

Consider the influences around you.

Are you surrounded by people you admire and respect?

Not people you *envy* but people that you admire and respect! People you look up to! People who have accomplished something or will in the future!

Do you have people in your life who have been blessed with the gift of wisdom? You will want to seek them out but remember, the best mentor that you could have is God!

So, put God first and everyone else after!

The influences around you now are more than likely the same kind of influences that you will have around your child!

Now is this a good choice?

NOTES

Consider seeking out a mentor.

If you cannot find a mentor in a real human being then consider finding a mentor in books to guide you toward a more rewarding and fulfilling life.

Be sure to add the Bible (King James) to your list of books as God has told us that he would never leave us nor forsake us and His is the only relationship that we can truly count on!

Find a mentor who will open your mind to learning and who will encourage you to be the best that you can possibly be!

Find a mentor who will encourage you to have a strong relationship with God as it is through God that we find our strength to meet all of life's challenges.

Now how beautiful is this?

NOTES

Consider the investment of time.

Be sure to explain all topics that come up at the different stages of your child's life.

I once read that children should learn of the world from adults and not from other children. This is so true!

Is it a wonder that so many young people are confused about life when nothing has been explained to them along the way?

How will they gain an understanding of right and wrong or respect and disrespect and the importance of a strong set of values, if everything is not explained to them along life's path?

Spending quality time with your children is so important!

NOTES

Consider developing who you are first.

Consider living life to its fullest and if you cannot afford to do everything that you would like, then read about it!

You would be surprised at how uplifting it can be to read about someone else's experiences!

Do you want to live your life for you? Or, do you want to live your life for this little being that you may bring into the world if you are not careful?

There is nothing wrong with wanting you to come first, maybe for the rest of your life or maybe for the next five or ten years!

Only you know the answer!

NOTES

Consider taking a good and honest look at yourself.

Look first at what you can give rather than what you can get from having a child!

Do you have a plan? Do you have a good education? Do you have a mentor or good role model? Will you further your education? Will you read several books on parenting before becoming a parent? Will you live your life Gods way meaning in righteousness?

Do you have a lot to offer in the way of love, as well as your time? Can you offer your child a tranquil and warm home environment?

Just a little more to think about!

NOTES

Consider looking at the heart.

Yes, his heart (the baby's father) and for you men, yes her heart.

Is it a heart filled with warmth and kindness, gentleness and understanding? Is it a heart filled with compassion and love for all?

Does she or he always have nice things to say about others? Why is this important? Because it is God's way!

Jesus said, "Love one another as I have loved thee" and "Love thy neighbor as thyself." How beautiful!

God says you can tell a man (no gender) by his kindness!

So guess what folks? It is what is in the heart that will either make or break your relationships!

NOTES

Consider marriage.

Chances are that right now you are too young to consider marriage and it is far better to get married first and have a child after. Why?

God said that to lie with a man (no gender) is to marry. Imagine!

Marriage should always come before having a child because it is a vow before God that you will spend the rest of your life with this woman or man!

After all, why help keep the divorce attorneys in business?

Now if you *think* about this, children are permanent but many marriages are not!

NOTES

Consider money.

Oh yes, money! Where will it come from? Will there be enough of it?

After all your living expenses are paid; an apartment, utilities, car expenses, insurance and food, will you have enough money left over to adequately care for your child?

Something to *think* about isn't it? There are thousands of books written on this one topic alone! Why? Unfortunately, everything we need to live comfortably requires money?

We work to earn money to keep a roof over our heads and to put food on our tables!

This is well worth thinking about as it (money) can cause such turmoil in a relationship so consider the money issue long term!

NOTES

Consider having more than one child.

I read something once that said, with one child comes a great deal of work and with two children comes ten times the work!

Children are smart! Boy! Oh boy! Do they know how to push your buttons!

After my late husband's death, I was so tired, lost and sad that I must say; parenting wore me down!

There were a few years when I signed my Christmas cards "Bonnie and Angels!"

Those who knew me well knew that this meant, things at home could have been much better!

How hard do you want to work? How tired do you want to be?

NOTES

Consider that in most cases it is the woman who raises the child.

We have read repeatedly about the numbers of struggling single mothers trying to make ends meet.

Raising a child is a full time commitment and a long term commitment! The work week feels longer and the week ends feel shorter!

I enjoy the court programs on television from time to time and am just astounded by all the young girls with children fathered by different men!

Some have two children by two different fathers or three children by three different fathers! Imagine!

NOTES

Consider starting a new relationship.

The child's father is not a part of your life any longer. How will your new partner handle your commitments to your child or your continuous contact with the child's father?

The phone calls may never stop because the child may keep you in each other's lives forever! Imagine the strain when you are trying to build a life with someone new!

It is so sad how far away from God we have fallen! I don't mean church! I mean the true word of God from the old bibles read by our elders!

Now girls and guys, *think* about how this child may keep the two of you bound to someone that you would rather not know!

NOTES

Consider delaying having a child until you have more to offer.

Consider not having a child unless you have been on your own for a while and have developed a strong sense of self or until you have completed your education beyond high school.

Consider self-education through the library and bookstores.

There are no guarantees in life! My dad always said the only two things we can count on are death and taxes, however, he did forget to mention God!

Read, read, read, and read every single book you can get your hands on that will help you with life's issues including a number of books that cover raising children!

NOTES

Consider the other parents past.

Did he or she come from a happy or unhappy home? Was there drinking or drugs? Was there anger, violence, or love, happiness and peace?

Was he or she raised with some advantages or was he or she raised in poverty?

Do you have similar morals or are they opposite of yours?

Consider the connection you two will have for the rest of your lives should you bring a child into the world!

Is this person, whether male or female, someone that you would want to keep in your life for the rest of your life?

You want someone who will enhance your life, not someone who will complicate it!

NOTES

Consider your level of patience.

Can you picture yourself asking the child five or more times to either do or not do something? This can be very frustrating!

There are children who behave badly for a number of reasons. If they are raised in an angry environment they often look for negative attention. Why?

They behave this way because their young mind believes that negative attention is better than no attention at all!

Children begin testing us early on and at times can seem relentless in pushing our buttons!

There are just so many forces in the world pulling us down that if we remember to *plan* and *think* and *adopt Godly ways*, we will all be much better off!

NOTES

Consider the disadvantages to living in poverty and not having enough money to pay your monthly expenses!

Yet you would bring a child into the world to live in poverty. Why?

If it is because you love children, wouldn't you want to provide a better life for yourself first and then for your child?

Though most of us are not wealthy, it is important for us as parents to do the best we can to see that our child fits in.

Now, I don't mean designer everything but I do mean your child should feel comfortable with the clothing they have for school.

It is important for our children to feel accepted and our job to help them get there!

NOTES

Consider how you will protect the child.

Keep in mind that the most difficult thing to do for a child is to protect him or her from the evils of the world and there are many!

Sometimes evil (meaning abuse) can exist under your own roof or in your own family without you ever suspecting a thing.

We are all aware now that there is a segment of the population that preys on children.

Predators come in all shapes and sizes and are not always strangers! They prey on the innocent and the unsuspecting and God is against it!

What precautions will you take to protect your children from the wicked world that we live in?

NOTES

.

Consider your reasons for having a child.

Sometimes women (or young women) especially have the need to nurture and sometimes even a desperate need to be needed!

This is not the reason to have a child! If this is what motivates you, consider getting a puppy!

At least if life does not unfold the way you had expected you are not committed to the puppy for twenty plus years!

Additionally, I have not heard of anyone being taken to court for puppy support!

Children are for the rest of your life and with that long term commitment you could become very tired!

NOTES

Young men, consider how you will feel about the child's mother if the relationship should end!

So many couples separate within the first five years after which you will be looking at twenty years of child support if you consider the college years.

How will it feel to hand this money over every single month for fifteen, eighteen or twenty years?

You may feel that you are paying the rent, car payment or the mortgage payment for your ex girlfriend and her new boyfriend or her new husband, even though child support is intended for the child!

It is just so sad that our values have deteriorated to the level that they have!

NOTES

Consider the repetitive schedule.

Consider waking up tired, going through the morning routine, getting the little one ready to be dropped off at daycare and getting yourself to work.

Work all day, pick up the child from daycare, cook, clean, go to bed and get up tired for five days in a row, four weeks a month and twelve months a year!

Do you think the work week will feel longer and the weekends shorter?

Life has many stresses whether due to raising a child, marriage, working full time or caring for pets, plants, a home and maintaining a car that runs, not to mention the money needed for rent, utilities etc.

These are just everyday stresses. Now add the stress associated with raising a child!

NOTES

Consider renting versus owning a home.

When renting, you may have to move because the landlord sold the property or because he needs the apartment for his son or brother!

The landlord may raise the rent to an amount that you cannot afford!

You may have to move because you got divorced, lost your roommate or boyfriend and you cannot afford the rent on your own!

Now consider adding a child to this scenario!

Moving a child or children from apartment to apartment is not what you would call offering a stable home environment!

NOTES

Consider taking charge of your life.

Read to learn and educate yourself to develop some life skills before bringing a child into the world!

Education alone can help to minimize the stress and frustration associated with raising a child as I once read that education is the ability to handle all of life's situations.

Always remember that knowledge is power while ignorance (not knowing) is vulnerability!

Open your eyes to the reality of all the obligations you will be faced with while raising a child.

Think about it! Work and children will pretty much run your life unless you give careful thought and planning to create a better life for you and your child!

NOTES

Consider the work.

It is not all fun! Raising children sometimes means being tugged at by a youngster who does not understand that sometimes adults need a break.

The work does not end. A work week of forty hours or more added to the time required to raise a child will cause you to need an endless supply of energy and patience.

The laundry, picking up the toys, the meals and giving the child the attention she or he is looking for just does not end.

Now, are you ready for this? Are you ready to make this long term commitment?

Have you been reading?

NOTES

Consider Welfare.

Were you raised on welfare? Were you proud of it if you were?

Were you ashamed? Is this what you would want for your child?

I am not knocking welfare and yes, it is a good thing if someone finds themselves in a bind, however, do your best *not* to adopt this lifestyle! Why? Your self esteem!

Remember, only one thing builds self-esteem and that is *accomplishment*!

While you have the time read! Don't forget, the library is free!

Put some knowledge in your mind so that you can have conversations worth having!

NOTES

Consider when you are sick.

Again, you cannot call in sick or take a day off from raising a child.

When you have a child, you no longer come first; regardless of how sick you are because the little one will be so dependent on you.

I got quite ill once and thank the Lord that my sister came to the house, fed my two children and got them off to school.

Then, they would take the bus to her house, she would feed them supper and then bring them home and get them ready for bed.

Although I was only hospitalized for about a week, I was quite ill for about a month.

What would I have done without her? She was such a blessing!

NOTES

Consider when you are tired.

You cannot punch out at five o'clock as you could from a job or be free to do what you want after school or work. You cannot say I need a day or two days off without considering the well-being of the child first.

You cannot walk in from work exhausted and take a nap, unless, the child is being cared for. You cannot stay in bed on a rainy Saturday morning escaping from all that is going on outside because the child will need your attention.

You do what needs to be done for your child and hope tomorrow will be a better day.

Consider the toll this may take on you while considering this long term!

NOTES

Consider your past.

Most often times children repeat the cycle of their upbringing, whether good or bad!

If you were raised in an environment with drinking and arguing, just keep in mind that you do not have to live the same way!

As you mature, you have the power to break the cycle to offer more to your child!

Just remember, the only way to break the cycle is to educate yourself and the idea is to be able to provide more for your children than was provided for you.

When you invest in yourself, you will be able to encourage your children to be the best that they can be!

NOTES

Consider that as parents we did the best we could.

Do you *think* we could have done even better had we considered what was involved long term and had we considered each of the points covered in this book as well as many others that are not covered?

Do you *think* we could have done better if our parents were more educated and therefore, we were encouraged to become educated in the home as well as outside of it?

I know I could have offered my children more opportunities had I taken the time to develop who I was first.

Therefore, I ask each of you to read this book with your friends and family and use the notes section to add your thoughts and comments.

Then I ask that you share this book with others to promote awareness and stimulating, thought provoking conversation regarding rearing a child.

NOTES

Consider having a close relationship with God as this is the most important seed that I could possibly share with you!

Talk to God and he will hear you. Do his work and he will bless you, while keeping in mind that He or She will not help you unless you *ask!*

God wants us to understand our changing world so we will be prepared and will not be afraid or confused by the increased wickedness all around us.

Surround yourself with kind people and *stay away* from gossip and negativity and do the best that you can to live your life God's way!

Before making any major decision always do your homework and consult with God!

There is power in prayer!

Ask questions, read, observe friends and strangers! Pay attention!

Collect some information and an understanding of what you are about to become involved with so you can then make an intelligent and more informed decision.

Do not do anything without God and remember:

A parent cannot teach a child what he or she has not yet learned!

Read and read some more! *Think* then act!

Consider the consequences to action without thought.

Think about your future!
Think about your education!
Think about your freedom!
Think about your environment!
Think about your finances!
Think about how easy or difficult you would like your life to be!
Think about how tired you want to be!
Think about who you are now and who you want to be in the future!
Think about what you can offer a child now as well as in the future!
Think about your long-term life plan.

How tired do I want to be?　.

Consider these seeds long term!

Ask yourself

How easy or difficult do I want my life to be?

How tired do I want to be?

Am I ready to devote twenty years or more of my life to this child?

Now Remember!

A parent cannot teach a child what he or she has not yet learned!

and

A child is for the rest of your life!

Think about the *truth* within the pages of this book. I learned more in two months of study with this chapel than I did going to church for ten years. Imagine!

To gain further understanding watch Shepherds Chapel daily for thirty days and make up your own mind and I believe you too will reach the same conclusion that I have, which is that this chapel teaches the word of God as God intended His word to be taught!

Call Shepherds Chapel
@ 1 800 643 4645

www.shepherdschapel.com

Call for this free tape (*a must have*) and viewing time in your area!

May God Bless you and your family now and always!

TITLES BY THIS AUTHOR

CONSIDER THIS
BEFORE
HAVING A CHILD

CONSIDER TRUTH
GOD'S TRUTH

CONSIDER EVERY WORD
OF
JESUS CHRIST
2 volumes

RAPTURE
FACT OR FICTION
YOU DECIDE